2020

January

M	T	W	T	F	S	S
		1	2	3	4	5
6	7	8	9	10	11	12
13	14	15	16	17	18	19
20	21	22	23	24	25	26
27	28	29	30	31		

February

M	T	W	T	F	S	S
					1	2
3	4	5	6	7	8	9
10	11	12	13	14	15	16
17	18	19	20	21	22	23
24	25	26	27	28	29	

March

M	T	W	T	F	S	S
						1
2	3	4	5	6	7	8
9	10	11	12	13	14	15
16	17	18	19	20	21	22
23	24	25	26	27	28	29
30	31					

April

M	T	W	T	F	S	S
	1	2	3	4	5	
6	7	8	9	10	11	12
13	14	15	16	17	18	19
20	21	22	23	24	25	26
27	28	29	30			

May

M	T	W	T	F	S	S
				1	2	3
4	5	6	7	8	9	10
11	12	13	14	15	16	17
18	19	20	21	22	23	24
25	26	27	28	29	30	31

June

M	T	W	T	F	S	S
1	2	3	4	5	6	7
8	9	10	11	12	13	14
15	16	17	18	19	20	21
22	23	24	25	26	27	28
29	30					

July

M	T	W	T	F	S	S
		1	2	3	4	5
6	7	8	9	10	11	12
13	14	15	16	17	18	19
20	21	22	23	24	25	26
27	28	29	30	31		

August

M	T	W	T	F	S	S
					1	2
3	4	5	6	7	8	9
10	11	12	13	14	15	16
17	18	19	20	21	22	23
24	25	26	27	28	29	30
31						

September

M	T	W	T	F	S	S
	1	2	3	4	5	6
7	8	9	10	11	12	13
14	15	16	17	18	19	20
21	22	23	24	25	26	27
28	29	30				

October

M	T	W	T	F	S	S
			1	2	3	4
5	6	7	8	9	10	11
12	13	14	15	16	17	18
19	20	21	22	23	24	25
26	27	28	29	30	31	

November

M	T	W	T	F	S	S
						1
2	3	4	5	6	7	8
9	10	11	12	13	14	15
16	17	18	19	20	21	22
23	24	25	26	27	28	29
30						

December

M	T	W	T	F	S	S
	1	2	3	4	5	6
7	8	9	10	11	12	13
14	15	16	17	18	19	20
21	22	23	24	25	26	27
28	29	30	31			

December

○ 30. MONDAY

REMINDERS

○ 31. TUESDAY

○ 1. WEDNESDAY

NOTES

○ 2. THURSDAY

○ 3. FRIDAY

○ 4. SATURDAY / 5. SUNDAY

January

○ 6. MONDAY

REMINDERS

○ 7. TUESDAY

○ 8. WEDNESDAY

NOTES

○ 9. THURSDAY

○ 10. FRIDAY

○ 11. SATURDAY / 12. SUNDAY

JANUARY

○ 13. MONDAY

REMINDERS

○ 14. TUESDAY

○ 15. WEDNESDAY

NOTES

○ 16. THURSDAY

○ 17. FRIDAY

○ 18. SATURDAY / 19. SUNDAY

JANUARY

○ 20. MONDAY

REMINDERS

○ 21. TUESDAY

○ 22. WEDNESDAY

NOTES

○ 23. THURSDAY

○ 24. FRIDAY

○ 25. SATURDAY / 26. SUNDAY

JANUARY

○ 27. MONDAY

REMINDERS

○ 28. TUESDAY

○ 29. WEDNESDAY

NOTES

○ 30. THURSDAY

○ 31. FRIDAY

○ 1. SATURDAY / 2. SUNDAY

FEBRUARY

○ 3. MONDAY

REMINDERS

○ 4. TUESDAY

○ 5. WEDNESDAY

NOTES

○ 6. THURSDAY

○ 7. FRIDAY

○ 8. SATURDAY / 9. SUNDAY

FEBRUARY

○ 10. MONDAY

REMINDERS

○ 11. TUESDAY

○ 12. WEDNESDAY

NOTES

○ 13. THURSDAY

○ 14. FRIDAY

○ 15. SATURDAY / 16. SUNDAY

FEBRUARY

○ 17. MONDAY

REMINDERS

○ 18. TUESDAY

○ 19. WEDNESDAY

NOTES

○ 20. THURSDAY

○ 21. FRIDAY

○ 22. SATURDAY / 23. SUNDAY

FEBRUARY

○ 24. MONDAY

REMINDERS

○ 25. TUESDAY

○ 26. WEDNESDAY

NOTES

○ 27. THURSDAY

○ 28. FRIDAY

○ 29. SATURDAY / 1. SUNDAY

MARCH

WEEK 10

○ 2. MONDAY

REMINDERS

○ 3. TUESDAY

○ 4. WEDNESDAY

NOTES

○ 5. THURSDAY

○ 6. FRIDAY

○ 7. SATURDAY / 8. SUNDAY

MARCH

○ 9. MONDAY

REMINDERS

○ 10. TUESDAY

○ 11. WEDNESDAY

NOTES

○ 12. THURSDAY

○ 13. FRIDAY

○ 14. SATURDAY / 15. SUNDAY

MARCH

○ 16. MONDAY

REMINDERS

○ 17. TUESDAY

○ 18. WEDNESDAY

NOTES

○ 19. THURSDAY

○ 20. FRIDAY

○ 21. SATURDAY / 22. SUNDAY

MARCH

○ 23. MONDAY

REMINDERS

○ 24. TUESDAY

○ 25. WEDNESDAY

NOTES

○ 26. THURSDAY

○ 27. FRIDAY

○ 28. SATURDAY / 29. SUNDAY

MARCH

○ 30. MONDAY

REMINDERS

○ 31. TUESDAY

○ 1. WEDNESDAY

NOTES

○ 2. THURSDAY

○ 3. FRIDAY

○ 4. SATURDAY / 5. SUNDAY

APRIL

○ 6. MONDAY

REMINDERS

○ 7. TUESDAY

○ 8. WEDNESDAY

NOTES

○ 9. THURSDAY

○ 10. FRIDAY

○ 11. SATURDAY / 12. SUNDAY

APRIL

○ 13. MONDAY

REMINDERS

○ 14. TUESDAY

○ 15. WEDNESDAY

NOTES

○ 16. THURSDAY

○ 17. FRIDAY

○ 18. SATURDAY / 19. SUNDAY

APRIL

○ 20. MONDAY

REMINDERS

○ 21. TUESDAY

○ 22. WEDNESDAY

NOTES

○ 23. THURSDAY

○ 24. FRIDAY

○ 25. SATURDAY / 26. SUNDAY

APRIL

○ 27. MONDAY

REMINDERS

○ 28. TUESDAY

○ 29. WEDNESDAY

NOTES

○ 30. THURSDAY

○ 1. FRIDAY

○ 2. SATURDAY / 3. SUNDAY

MAY

○ 4. MONDAY

REMINDERS

○ 5. TUESDAY

○ 6. WEDNESDAY

NOTES

○ 7. THURSDAY

○ 8. FRIDAY

○ 9. SATURDAY / 10. SUNDAY

MAY

WEEK 20

○ 11. MONDAY

REMINDERS

○ 12. TUESDAY

○ 13. WEDNESDAY

NOTES

○ 14. THURSDAY

○ 15. FRIDAY

○ 16. SATURDAY / 17. SUNDAY

MAY

WEEK 21

○ 18. MONDAY

○ 19. TUESDAY

○ 20. WEDNESDAY

○ 21. THURSDAY

○ 22. FRIDAY

○ 23. SATURDAY / 24. SUNDAY

REMINDERS

NOTES

MAY

○ 25. MONDAY

REMINDERS

○ 26. TUESDAY

○ 27. WEDNESDAY

NOTES

○ 28. THURSDAY

○ 29. FRIDAY

○ 30. SATURDAY / 31. SUNDAY

JUNE

○ 1. MONDAY

REMINDERS

○ 2. TUESDAY

○ 3. WEDNESDAY

NOTES

○ 4. THURSDAY

○ 5. FRIDAY

○ 6. SATURDAY / 7. SUNDAY

JUNE

WEEK 24

○ 8. MONDAY

REMINDERS

○ 9. TUESDAY

○ 10. WEDNESDAY

NOTES

○ 11. THURSDAY

○ 12. FRIDAY

○ 13. SATURDAY / 14. SUNDAY

JUNE

○ 15. MONDAY

REMINDERS

○ 16. TUESDAY

○ 17. WEDNESDAY

NOTES

○ 18. THURSDAY

○ 19. FRIDAY

○ 20. SATURDAY / 21. SUNDAY

June

○ 22. MONDAY

REMINDERS

○ 23. TUESDAY

○ 24. WEDNESDAY

NOTES

○ 25. THURSDAY

○ 26. FRIDAY

○ 27. SATURDAY / 28. SUNDAY

JUNE

○ 29. MONDAY

REMINDERS

○ 30. TUESDAY

○ 1. WEDNESDAY

NOTES

○ 2. THURSDAY

○ 3. FRIDAY

○ 4. SATURDAY / 5. SUNDAY

JULY

○ 6. MONDAY

REMINDERS

○ 7. TUESDAY

○ 8. WEDNESDAY

NOTES

○ 9. THURSDAY

○ 10. FRIDAY

○ 11. SATURDAY / 12. SUNDAY

JULY
WEEK 29

○ 13. MONDAY

REMINDERS

○ 14. TUESDAY

○ 15. WEDNESDAY

NOTES

○ 16. THURSDAY

○ 17. FRIDAY

○ 18. SATURDAY / 19. SUNDAY

JULY
WEEK 30

○ 20. MONDAY

○ 21. TUESDAY

○ 22. WEDNESDAY

○ 23. THURSDAY

○ 24. FRIDAY

○ 25. SATURDAY / 26. SUNDAY

REMINDERS

NOTES

JULY

WEEK 31

○ 27. MONDAY

○ 28. TUESDAY

○ 29. WEDNESDAY

○ 30. THURSDAY

○ 31. FRIDAY

○ 1. SATURDAY / 2. SUNDAY

REMINDERS

NOTES

AUGUST

WEEK 32

○ 3. MONDAY

REMINDERS

○ 4. TUESDAY

○ 5. WEDNESDAY

NOTES

○ 6. THURSDAY

○ 7. FRIDAY

○ 8. SATURDAY / 9. SUNDAY

August

Week 33

○ 10. MONDAY

REMINDERS

○ 11. TUESDAY

○ 12. WEDNESDAY

NOTES

○ 13. THURSDAY

○ 14. FRIDAY

○ 15. SATURDAY / 16. SUNDAY

AUGUST

○ 17. MONDAY

REMINDERS

○ 18. TUESDAY

○ 19. WEDNESDAY

NOTES

○ 20. THURSDAY

○ 21. FRIDAY

○ 22. SATURDAY / 23. SUNDAY

AUGUST

○ 24. MONDAY

REMINDERS

○ 25. TUESDAY

○ 26. WEDNESDAY

NOTES

○ 27. THURSDAY

○ 28. FRIDAY

○ 29. SATURDAY / 30. SUNDAY

AUGUST

○ 31. MONDAY

○ 1. TUESDAY

○ 2. WEDNESDAY

○ 3. THURSDAY

○ 4. FRIDAY

○ 5. SATURDAY / 6. SUNDAY

REMINDERS

NOTES

SEPTEMBER

○ 7. MONDAY

REMINDERS

○ 8. TUESDAY

○ 9. WEDNESDAY

NOTES

○ 10. THURSDAY

○ 11. FRIDAY

○ 12. SATURDAY / 13. SUNDAY

SEPTEMBER

○ 14. MONDAY

REMINDERS

○ 15. TUESDAY

○ 16. WEDNESDAY

NOTES

○ 17. THURSDAY

○ 18. FRIDAY

○ 19. SATURDAY / 20. SUNDAY

SEPTEMBER

○ 21. MONDAY

REMINDERS

○ 22. TUESDAY

○ 23. WEDNESDAY

NOTES

○ 24. THURSDAY

○ 25. FRIDAY

○ 26. SATURDAY / 27. SUNDAY

SEPTEMBER

○ 28. MONDAY

REMINDERS

○ 29. TUESDAY

○ 30. WEDNESDAY

NOTES

○ 1. THURSDAY

○ 2. FRIDAY

○ 3. SATURDAY / 4. SUNDAY

OCTOBER

○ 5. MONDAY

REMINDERS

○ 6. TUESDAY

○ 7. WEDNESDAY

NOTES

○ 8. THURSDAY

○ 9. FRIDAY

○ 10. SATURDAY / 11. SUNDAY

OCTOBER

WEEK 42

○ 12. MONDAY

REMINDERS

_____

○ 13. TUESDAY

_____

○ 14. WEDNESDAY

NOTES

_____

○ 15. THURSDAY

_____

○ 16. FRIDAY

_____

○ 17. SATURDAY / 18. SUNDAY

_____

OCTOBER

○ 19. MONDAY

REMINDERS

○ 20. TUESDAY

○ 21. WEDNESDAY

NOTES

○ 22. THURSDAY

○ 23. FRIDAY

○ 24. SATURDAY / 25. SUNDAY

OCTOBER

○ 26. MONDAY

REMINDERS

○ 27. TUESDAY

○ 28. WEDNESDAY

NOTES

○ 29. THURSDAY

○ 30. FRIDAY

○ 31. SATURDAY / 1. SUNDAY

November

○ 2. MONDAY

REMINDERS

○ 3. TUESDAY

○ 4. WEDNESDAY

NOTES

○ 5. THURSDAY

○ 6. FRIDAY

○ 7. SATURDAY / 8. SUNDAY

November

○ 9. MONDAY

REMINDERS

○ 10. TUESDAY

○ 11. WEDNESDAY

NOTES

○ 12. THURSDAY

○ 13. FRIDAY

○ 14. SATURDAY / 15. SUNDAY

November

○ 16. MONDAY

REMINDERS

○ 17. TUESDAY

○ 18. WEDNESDAY

NOTES

○ 19. THURSDAY

○ 20. FRIDAY

○ 21. SATURDAY / 22. SUNDAY

November

○ 23. MONDAY

REMINDERS

○ 24. TUESDAY

○ 25. WEDNESDAY

NOTES

○ 26. THURSDAY

○ 27. FRIDAY

○ 28. SATURDAY / 29. SUNDAY

November

○ 30. MONDAY

○ 1. TUESDAY

○ 2. WEDNESDAY

○ 3. THURSDAY

○ 4. FRIDAY

○ 5. SATURDAY / 6. SUNDAY

REMINDERS

NOTES

December

○ 7. MONDAY

REMINDERS

○ 8. TUESDAY

○ 9. WEDNESDAY

NOTES

○ 10. THURSDAY

○ 11. FRIDAY

○ 12. SATURDAY / 13. SUNDAY

December

○ 14. MONDAY

REMINDERS

○ 15. TUESDAY

○ 16. WEDNESDAY

NOTES

○ 17. THURSDAY

○ 18. FRIDAY

○ 19. SATURDAY / 20. SUNDAY

December

○ 21. MONDAY

REMINDERS

○ 22. TUESDAY

○ 23. WEDNESDAY

NOTES

○ 24. THURSDAY

○ 25. FRIDAY

○ 26. SATURDAY / 27. SUNDAY

December

○ 28. MONDAY

REMINDERS

○ 29. TUESDAY

○ 30. WEDNESDAY

NOTES

○ 31. THURSDAY

○ 1. FRIDAY

○ 2. SATURDAY / 3. SUNDAY

2021

January

M	T	W	T	F	S	S
				1	2	3
4	5	6	7	8	9	10
11	12	13	14	15	16	17
18	19	20	21	22	23	24
25	26	27	28	29	30	31

February

M	T	W	T	F	S	S
1	2	3	4	5	6	7
8	9	10	11	12	13	14
15	16	17	18	19	20	21
22	23	24	25	26	27	28

March

M	T	W	T	F	S	S
1	2	3	4	5	6	7
8	9	10	11	12	13	14
15	16	17	18	19	20	21
22	23	24	25	26	27	28
29	30	31				

April

M	T	W	T	F	S	S
			1	2	3	4
5	6	7	8	9	10	11
12	13	14	15	16	17	18
19	20	21	22	23	24	25
26	27	28	29	30		

May

M	T	W	T	F	S	S
					1	2
3	4	5	6	7	8	9
10	11	12	13	14	15	16
17	18	19	20	21	22	23
24	25	26	27	28	29	30
31						

June

M	T	W	T	F	S	S
	1	2	3	4	5	6
7	8	9	10	11	12	13
14	15	16	17	18	19	20
21	22	23	24	25	26	27
28	29	30				

July

M	T	W	T	F	S	S
			1	2	3	4
5	6	7	8	9	10	11
12	13	14	15	16	17	18
19	20	21	22	23	24	25
26	27	28	29	30	31	

August

M	T	W	T	F	S	S
						1
2	3	4	5	6	7	8
9	10	11	12	13	14	15
16	17	18	19	20	21	22
23	24	25	26	27	28	29
30	31					

September

M	T	W	T	F	S	S
		1	2	3	4	5
6	7	8	9	10	11	12
13	14	15	16	17	18	19
20	21	22	23	24	25	26
27	28	29	30			

October

M	T	W	T	F	S	S
				1	2	3
4	5	6	7	8	9	10
11	12	13	14	15	16	17
18	19	20	21	22	23	24
25	26	27	28	29	30	31

November

M	T	W	T	F	S	S
1	2	3	4	5	6	7
8	9	10	11	12	13	14
15	16	17	18	19	20	21
22	23	24	25	26	27	28
29	30					

December

M	T	W	T	F	S	S
		1	2	3	4	5
6	7	8	9	10	11	12
13	14	15	16	17	18	19
20	21	22	23	24	25	26
27	28	29	30	31		

Printed in Great Britain
by Amazon